WHAT ARE YOUR CHANCES OF BEING ATTACKED?

What is your chance of being psychically attacked at some point in your life? Fairly high, evidence suggests. This does not mean that you will be victimized in a dramatic, life-threatening way, but it is very likely that at some time or another you will incur the wrath of someone whose anger will find paranormal expression, whether your attacker realizes it or not. Sometimes this fierce, concentrated anger can attract evil energy, trigger malevolent psychokinesis or induce sickness. Ours is an intensely stressful, violent, and competitive age. There is much pollution in our psychic environment, and that includes those who use their power for destructive ends.

The key to psychic self-defense lies in knowing how to strengthen your life force to withstand the daily barrage of negative energy hitting you. With exercises that awaken your "psychic muscles," and techniques that bolster your energy, fear from the reality of outside aggression and manipulation diminishes.

The Truth About Psychic Self-Defense explains how to employ your own positive energies to gain control and security in your life. You will establish unbreakable contact with your Higher Self: the source of all psychic well-being.

LLEWELLYN'S VANGUARD SERIES

The Truth About

Psychic Self-Defense

by Keith Randolph

1995
Llewellyn Publications
St. Paul, MN 55164-0383, U.S.A.

FIRST EDITION (Titled *The Truth About Psychic Attack*), 1984
Second Printing, 1987
SECOND EDITION (Titled *The Truth About Psychic Self-Defense*), 1989
Second Printing, 1993
THIRD EDITION
First Printing, 1995

Cover illustration by Anne Marie Garrison

International Standard Book Number:
0-87542-352-3

LLEWELLYN PUBLICATIONS
A Division of Llewellyn Worldwide, Ltd.
P.O. Box 64383, St. Paul, MN 55164-0383

THE TRUTH ABOUT PSYCHIC SELF-DEFENSE

INTRODUCTION

Are you vulnerable to psychic attack?

The answer, in all likelihood, is *yes*. You are immune to psychic attack only if you have learned how to protect yourself from this kind of assault—and most people don't even know psychic attack is possible, much less that they can learn techniques of psychic self-defense to protect themselves from such supernatural assault.

There was a time in the history of Western civilization when psychic attack was a major concern in the lives of many people. Almost any misfortune could be attributed to the malevolent activities of a local "witch," real or imagined, whose ability to manipulate magical energies for harmful purposes was assumed by all but a tiny minority of skeptical rationalists. Even today, in so-called "primitive" societies, considerable time and effort are devoted to preserving oneself against depredations by sorcerers or evil spirits.

Clearly there is a considerable amount of superstitious nonsense surrounding the idea of supernatural assault. Some people who believe they are psychic-attack victims are, in reality, in urgent need of psychiatric attention. The voices they hear in their heads are probably *not* the voices of evil elementals.

But all of us, including those of us who are neither superstitious nor paranoid, have at one time or another had the experience of meeting a person who seemed somehow to drain the very life force from us. Even in brief, casual encounters the effect of this kind of "psychic vampirism" is intense and unmistakable. And if our acquaintance with the person extends over a period of time, we may suffer serious consequences: not only an energy drain, but a sense that this person is exercising undue influence over our lives, and not for the good. We may find ourselves engaged in a fierce battle of wills, fearing that if we lose, we will sacrifice our identities as individuals. Yet curiously, this dramatic and frightening combat often takes place on a level that is not vocally acknowledged, either by us or by the person directing the psychic attack against us!

The attacker may be someone with an amoral bent combined with a kind of warped personal magnetism and may not be fully conscious of his power, which is just as well. But if he *is* conscious of that power, and knows the techniques necessary to focus it for maximum effect, he is an extraordinarily dangerous individual—because then he is drawing on not only psychological forces but paranormal ones as well. In that case his victims can find themselves in very serious trouble indeed. It is one thing to fight an enemy who uses conventional emotional weapons; it is quite another to find oneself at the receiving end of malevolent "supernatural" forces whose existence one may not suspect until it is too late.

The Truth About Psychic Self-Defense is an examination of the varieties of paranormal assault: who commits it, how it works, whom it affects, and what its victims have done about it. We believe in the ancient principle that forewarned is forearmed—unless you know what *can* (and probably *will*) happen to you, you can't do anything to protect yourself. In this, as in all matters, ignorance is dangerous. Knowledge is the beginning not only of wisdom but of strength. From strength and wisdom come the power to withstand the forces of pure evil unleashed in psychic attacks.

Now let us enter the valley of the shadow ... .

SUPERNATURAL ASSAULT

Some years ago an English colonial official stationed at a remote post on a Caribbean island became seriously ill from a cause the district medical officer could not determine. The official asked to be transferred elsewhere, saying he was sure he would die if forced to remain where he was. His superiors refused his request, but the man's health continued to deteriorate and he grew seriously depressed. Again he asked to be transferred. This time he said he would leave the foreign service entirely if his plea was denied. He got the transfer and recovered his health as soon as he left the area.

A year and a half later another local official experienced a slight attack of fever. But no sooner had he shaken that off than he found he was suffering from an inexplicable melancholy. Strangely, however, the depression would leave him once he had passed a certain distance from his residence. On his return, as he neared his residence, it felt as if a wet blanket were being thrown over him, and he would lapse again into severe depression. When his physical health began to deteriorate, he asked to be transferred.

Shortly after his departure, the district medical officer's wife, who lived in the same area, became afflicted with depression and ill health. Because she had always been a cheerful, healthy woman, her husband and friends were perplexed and alarmed.

One night at midnight she woke up screaming. When her husband rushed into the room, she said she had awakened in a state of fearsome depression. Her eyes fell on a large and hideous form moving through the room. She described it as something between a spider and a jellyfish. Although she insisted she had seen this creature in a waking state, her husband assumed, not unreasonably, that she had had a nightmare.

When the same thing happened the next night, however, the doctor began to sense that he and his wife were confronting an eerie, evil, and very real force. After the second visitation the woman's health collapsed entirely. In the morning she told her husband that she had to leave or she would die.

He agreed to take her on a week-long vacation. He was sure this would cheer her up, and it did. But when they got back, her black depression immediately returned.

IDENTIFYING A VAMPIRE

A few nights later the woman again woke up screaming. Her husband found her in a weakened state, but able to make a curious request. "I want you to examine the back of my neck and shoulders very carefully and see if there is any mark on the skin of any kind whatever," she said.

The doctor looked without success. But his wife was insistent. "Get a glass and look again," she said. "See if you can find any puncture from a sharp pointed tooth." Again he found nothing. Finally the woman explained why she had asked him to conduct the examination:

"I dreamed that I was in a house where I lived when I was a little girl. My little boy called out to me. I ran down to him but when I reached the bottom of the stairs, a tall black man came toward me. I waved him off, but I could not move to get away from him, though I pushed the boy out of his reach. The man came toward me, seized me in his arms, sat down at the bottom of the stairs, put me on his knee and proceeded to suck from a point at the upper part of the spine, just below the neck. I felt that he was drawing all the blood and life out of me. Then he threw me from himself, and apparently I lost consciousness as he did so. I felt as though I was dying. Then I woke up and I had been lying here for a quarter of an hour or 20 minutes before I was able to call you."

The next morning she told her husband, "I have a feeling, somehow, that it will not happen again. I feel quite well and strong and all my depression is gone."

That afternoon the couple were on their way to a social engagement when suddenly the woman stopped. Her eyes focused on a tall Indian farmer, a man who owned a large herd of milk cattle and who was reputed to be quite wealthy. "That is the man I saw in my dream," she declared.

The doctor walked up to the man and said, "I know everything that happened last night at midnight." He threatened to kill the farmer if he did not leave the area in 12 hours.

The farmer was gone by evening, departing so hurriedly that he left behind his cattle and the money in his bank account. "No news had been heard of him five years afterwards," Dudley Wright reported in an article on the case in *Occult Review* (July 1910). "Since his departure no one has complained of depression and lassitude in that area."

PSYCHIC ATTACK

Could a story like this be true?

We who live in an age of science, reason, and materialism are likely to sit back and smile smugly when we hear such tales. We can easily tell ourselves that the Westerners who thought they were victimized by this kind of "psychic vampirism" simply fell prey to native superstition and suffered from psychosomatic illnesses.

The belief that certain persons possess malevolent supernatural powers they may use to harm others is ancient. It underlay the widespread fear in medieval Europe that "witches" and sorcerers were causing misfortunes of all kinds. In a famous (or notorious) seventeenth century book on witchcraft, Francesco-Maria Guazzo's *Compendium Maleficarum*, the symptoms of witch attack are said to include:

> Loss of appetite
> Intense pain in the heart
> Impotence
> Discomfort in the neck, kidneys, or belly
> Yellowing of skin
> Inability to look a priest in the eye
> Sweating even in cold weather
> Stomach disorders

"The sicknesses with which those who are bewitched suffer," Guazzo wrote, "are generally a wasting or emaciation of the whole body and a loss of strength, together with a deep languor, dullness of mind, various melancholy ravings, different kinds of fever ... certain convulsive movements of an epileptic appearance; a sort of rigidity of the limbs giving the appearance of a fit; sometimes ... such a weakness pervades the whole body that [victims] can hardly move on any account at all ... If by chance the witch should come to see the sick man, the patient is at once affected with great uneasiness and seized with terror and trembling. If it is a child, it cries."

FIGHTING OFF A PSYCHIC ATTACK

The story a man named Antonio Vega tells could have come out of the Middle Ages, but it is supposed to have happened in California in 1973. Vega recounts his terrifying experience in the January 1977 issue of *Fate* magazine, published by Llewellyn Publications.

On February 17, 1973, Vega writes, he received a call from his brother, Ernesto, who said he was suffering from severe abdominal pains and was going to the hospital the next day for tests and possible surgery. When the tests were completed, Ernesto told his brother that the doctors still didn't know what his problem was. They decided to try exploratory surgery, which also failed to determine the cause of this suffering.

The pain continued and within days Ernesto Vega was dead. Even after they had conducted an autopsy, the doctors were still puzzled about the mysterious, fatal illness which had so suddenly struck a man in excellent health. They finally decided, unhelpfully to the grieving family, that Ernesto had died of an "undetermined illness."

Six months later, Antonio Vega's health began to give out. He suffered sudden and intense dizzy spells which made him feel as if he were floating on air. His mouth and throat were always inexplicably dry—and, most ominously, he was racked by excruciating abdominal pain. The pain was so overwhelming that Vega could hardly eat; the mere intake of food increased the already unbearable discomfort.

As had his late brother, Vega sought medical help, but without success. Finally his doctor could only conclude that his illness was psychosomatic. He referred the desperately sick man to an internist and to a psychiatrist. They were baffled, too.

When Vega's mother-in-law, Leonora Perez, suggested a supernatural cause—a psychic attack by someone who hated him—Vega scoffed. But his wife and her mother were so worried about him that at last he consented to go to a Los Angeles *brujo* (a wizard, conjurer or sorcerer), Joe Mendez. The women were convinced that the *brujo* could help Vega. At that point, Vega, remembering what had happened to his brother, felt he had nothing to lose. On May 30, 1974, his wife, Sue, called Mendez and set up an appointment for the next morning.

"YOUR HUSBAND IS *ENBRUJADO*"

Mendez went to work immediately. The next day, when Vega, his wife, and mother-in-law called on him, he claimed someone had cast a spell on him. He said, "The person has performed it little by little, to make it seem a natural illness that would eventually lead to your death. I know that you feel this is nonsense, but you will see, you will believe. I can't tell you who has done this to you, Tony, but you will know eventually."

The *brujo* had Vega step into a room where he performed a ritual, which he said would restore the afflicted man's vitality. Vega didn't believe it, especially when he felt no better the rest of that day or the next. At the end of the second day, as the couple retired for the night, Sue looked startled. "I thought I heard someone whisper in my ear," she said. The "voice" had said, "Your husband is *enbrujado*, and he will get well."

Suddenly Sue passed out, leaving Vega to suffer the terrible pains alone. His abdominal pains were so intense that he could scarcely breathe. He felt as if he were on fire.

Finally Vega hobbled to his feet, hoping fresh air would give him some relief. His dogs growled menacingly at him, treating him like a total stranger. When he called them by name, they grew even more unfriendly.

He struggled back to bed and desperately began to pray. Just then he heard a whistling noise and something smacked against the table next to his bed. At that moment the pain left him. His body seemed to rise, and he started shaking so badly that the bed vibrated. Something like an explosion sounded from the kitchen. He wondered if the house were caving in.

Just as he started to relax, there was another "explosion." His body shook again. He sensed the presence of someone, a protector, leaning over him but he could see no one.

The last explosion occurred in the corner of the bedroom and it woke his wife, who bolted upright shouting, "My God! What was that?"

The rest of the night passed peacefully.

THE ATTACKER

The next morning, a Sunday, the Vegas and their children dressed for Mass. On their way to church they decided to call on Sue's mother to tell her what had happened during the night.

As the couple turned the corner on the way to her house, Mr. Vega's eyes were suddenly afflicted with a burning sensation. And as they greeted Mrs. Perez, his body was consumed in something like an invisible flame. The pain was back with a vengeance. He was too uncomfortable to go to church. He stayed with his mother-in-law until his wife and children returned from the service.

As soon as they got back home, Tony lay down. Something seemed to be hitting him in the stomach, and he kept hearing noises like chanting voices and rocks crashing against the window. For 72 hours he could neither eat nor sleep.

Early Tuesday morning Sue called Joe Mendez, the *brujo*, to let him know what was going on. "They do not want to release you," he said. "If it's a fight they want, they shall have it and they will lose. But I must see you once more."

Two hours later the couple set out for Los Angeles. Tony lay in the back seat praying and fearing he would die before they got to their destination. Meanwhile, Sue was fighting her own battle. A few miles down the road she had developed a splitting headache and something kept telling her to fall asleep. She had to struggle to stay awake, all the while cursing whoever or whatever was trying to destroy her and her husband.

Somehow they made it to Mendez's place. When he saw how ill Sue was, he told her, "They were trying to keep you from getting Tony here. Please come in. I will take care of both of you immediately."

An hour later the two emerged from the house feeling completely well. Three days afterwards Tony met with his psychiatrist, who was puzzled by his sudden cure. His only explanation was, "Faith can help a lot of people and yours has cured you."

The following week, as Tony was entering the hallway of his house, he was startled by the apparitional form of a large, fat woman. He recognized it immediately as his dead brother's wife.

"You saw the woman who wanted to kill you, as she did her husband," Mendez explained. "The woman is your sister-in-law. I could not tell you this before, for it is against our ethics, but you saw her and now you do believe."

THE REALITY OF PSYCHIC ATTACK

In one sense, we are all victims of psychic attack. We're psychically assaulted almost constantly by a world that has little respect for our precious selves and that seeks to influence and manipulate us in all kinds of ways, some of them potentially harmful.

In the twentieth century, we have seen the institutionalization of psychic attack in the rise of totalitarian political systems. In such states, individual human beings exist only to be manipulated into "acceptable" patterns of thinking and behaving. In assuming total control of the educational system, the mass media, the arts, popular culture, science, the courts, and the police, rulers of totalitarian nations seek to exercise utter domination of even the most private aspects of citizens' lives.

Those of us fortunate enough to live in more benign and democratic nations are still subject to psychic assault, though not quite so obviously or savagely as those who dwell in police states. "Madison Avenue" (the advertising and public relations industry) for example, works unceasingly to persuade us to buy things we could well do without. Using sophisticated techniques of psychological manipulation, it plays on insecurities, prejudices, and vanities we may not even consciously realize we possess. Politicians play on these same human weaknesses, hoping to manipulate us into pulling the proper levers in the voting booths, or to make us believe it is in our best interests to fight in wars in obscure, distant countries.

Simply by virtue of the fact that we are human beings interacting with other human beings, we find our sense of selfhood subject to attack, often in subtle fashion. Friends and relatives try to get us to do things we may not wish to do. Those who consciously wish us ill may assault our egos, our feelings of pride and worth, and our good names.

To survive in a world that is in its best moments vexing and in its worst downright frightening, we learn to develop techniques of psychic self-defense. If we do not learn how to protect ourselves, if we cannot maintain some control over our own souls and circumstances, we become mere shells. Not only our mental health collapses; recent scientific and medical research tells us that our physical health can be imperiled as well. People who let themselves become overwhelmed by the world may unconsciously will themselves to die. For example, cancer researchers believe that some instances of the disease are psychologically rooted in the victims' sense of their own helplessness.

The reality of these kinds of "normal" psychic attacks is disputed by no one. But our rational minds rebel at the thought of paranormal psychic attacks, although they are alleged to have occurred throughout human history, even as we have seen—in late twentieth-century America.

TERROR IN THE NIGHT

Yet psychic attacks inexplicable in terms of twentieth-century scientific knowledge occur far more frequently than most of us would imagine. A study conducted by Dr. David J. Hufford, a behavioral scientist at the Pennsylvania State College of Medicine, has brought to light the unsettling fact that one American in every six has had the following experience at one time or another:

Typically the victim suddenly awakens in the middle of the night, and is shocked to discover that he or she is unable to move. The victim is certain that he or she is awake and not simply suffering an unpleasant dream. As he or she lies there, immobilized and vulnerable, the victim hears footsteps and suddenly sees a hideous, ghostlike form that seems to exude evil. An invisible force presses down on the chest, and the horrified victim thinks he or she is going to die. Then, as abruptly as it arrived, the paralysis leaves. The apparition vanishes and the individual feels normal.

Sometimes poltergeist-like manifestations accompany the attack. Other apparitions may appear, and other strange events may occur. But in most instances these weird night entities attack on their own, leaving the victim shaken, scared—and silent.

As a social scientist, Hufford, who reported his research in a fascinating book entitled *The Terror That Comes in the Night* (University of Pennsylvania Press, 1982), was especially interested in this last aspect of the phenomenon. Like most Americans, Hufford had never heard of such night attacks, until, as a college student, one happened to him. He thought he was suffering some dire illness, or sensing the first signs of mental derangement, until he did some research on the subject.

He learned that while these experiences are so little spoken of in this country we don't even have a name for them, other cultures recognize the phenomenon and identify it in various ways. In Newfoundland it is known as the "Old Hag,""The Hags,"or "Hagging." The terms hark back to an old belief that these are witch attacks, "witches" traditionally depicted as ugly old women or hags. A victim of hagging was thought to be hag- or witch-ridden. In fact, the most common word in English for the experience is "riding."

But the original name, interestingly enough, is one with which we are all familiar: nightmare.

INCUBUS AND SUCCUBUS

To us, the word "nightmare" has come to mean nothing more than "bad dream," but traditionally it had a far more specific definition. It referred to an incubus or succubus which came in the night to place a crushing weight on a sleeper's breast. Earnest Jones, a famous psychoanalyst and biographer of Freud, explains:

> The word Nightmare itself comes from the Anglo-Saxon nicht (night) and mara (incubus or succubus). The Anglo-Saxon suffix a denotes an agent, so that mara from the verb merran, literally means a 'crusher,' and the connotation of a crushing weight on the breast is common to the corresponding word in allied language (Icelandic mara, Danish mare, Low German moore, Bohemian mara, Swedish mara, Old High German mara) ... From the earliest times the oppressing agency experienced during sleep was personified.

For example, in a 1597 work entitled *Daemonologie*, two fictitious characters debate the reality of witchcraft and, in the quoted passage below, the cause of night attacks:

> Philomates: It is not the thing which we call the Mare, which takes folkes sleeping in their beds, a kinde of these spirits, whereof ye are speaking?

> Epistemon: No, that is but a natural sickness, which the Mediciners have given that name of Incubus unto, ab incubando, because it ... makes us think that there were some unnatural burden or spirit, lying upon us, and holding us down.

A twentieth-century instance of such a supernatural night attack took place in 1915, according to an account collected in Newfoundland by folklorists investigating the subject. It came about, the informant told the investigators, because of a love triangle.

A man named Robert was trying to date Jean, who was John's girlfriend. About a month into this state of affairs, Robert began to suffer from a strange and terrifying problem. Every night when he would go to bed, it felt as if someone were crushing his chest and trying to strangle him. He became so sick that those who knew him thought he was going to die.

Then an old man Robert knew placed a board over his chest and put an opened pocketknife in his hands. That way, the "hag" who was trying to kill him would herself be killed.

But when Robert woke up in the morning, he was alarmed to see the knife sticking into the piece of board—suggesting that the weapon would have been plunged into his heart had the wood not stopped it. That, however, proved to be the last attack.

Robert assumed that John, jealous of Robert's attempts to steal away his lady friend, had called the hag. Robert said he always heard the hag coming, and could even see it (he would say only that it looked "human"). Robert could not escape the hag because whenever it appeared he became paralyzed.

"SOMETHING WAS PRESENT"

Another striking example of a hag encounter is described in William James' classic *The Varieties of Religious Experience* (1902). James describes the man who had the experiences as "an intimate friend ... one of the keenest intellects I know."

It was about September 1884, when I had the first experience. James' friend reported:

> On the previous night I had had, after getting into bed at my rooms in College, a vivid tactile hallucination of being grasped by the arm, which made me get up and search the room for an intruder; but the sense of presence ... came on the next night. After I had got into bed and blown out the candle, I lay awake thinking on the previous night's experience, when suddenly I felt something come into the room and stay close to my bed. It remained only a minute or two. I did not recognize it by any ordinary sense, and yet there was a horribly unpleasant 'sensation' connected with it. It stirred something more at the roots of my being than any ordinary perception. The feeling had something of the quality of a large

tearing vital pain spreading chiefly over the chest, but within the organism—and yet the feeling was not pain so much as abhorrence. At all events, something was present with me, and I knew its presence far more surely than I have ever known the presence of any fleshly living creature. I was as conscious of its departure as of its coming: an almost instantaneously swift going through the door, and the 'horrible sensation' disappeared.

On the third night when I retired, my mind was absorbed in some lectures which I was preparing, and I was still absorbed in these when I became aware of the actual presence (though not of the coming) of the thing that was there the night before, and of the 'horrible sensation.' I then mentally concentrated all my effort to charge this 'thing,' if it was evil, to depart, if it was not evil, to tell me who or what it was, and if it could not explain itself, to go, and that I would compel it to go. It went as on the previous night, and my body quickly recovered its normal state.

On two other occasions in my life, I have had precisely the same 'horrible sensation.' Once it lasted a full quarter of an hour. In all three instances, something was present which felt stronger than the feeling of being around ordinary people. The feeling of something seemed close to me and intensely more real than any ordinary perception. Although I felt it to be like myself, so to speak, or finite, small, and distressful, as it were, I didn't recognize it as any individual being or person.

SOMETHING WICKED
THIS WAY COMES ...

A different kind of psychic attack occurred in 1969 in New Jersey, and its victim was a frail 2½-year-old boy named Peter Blair McDonald.

Peter had come into the world with a terrible variety of physical imperfections, chief among them vital organs (including heart, liver, and spleen) that were too large for his little body. For months doctors feared he could die at any time. Somehow he managed to survive and at length his health, though still somewhat precarious, improved. He was on his way to starting a normal life when an evil, paranormal entity decided it wanted to kill him.

At 2:00 A.M. one night in the spring of 1969, Peter's mother, Martha McDonald, was awakened by her son's hysterical screams. When she rushed into his room, she felt a sharp, damp coldness which seemed to cut right through her. The air was strangely heavy, and Mrs. McDonald had the distinct, uneasy sensation that someone besides herself, Peter, and Peter's older brother (still sleeping) was in the room—someone she could not see.

As his mother held the shaking little boy, he told her that a "man" was standing in the room and staring at him. He had been awakened, he said, by the sound of scratching at his window. When he looked, he saw a form standing near him. He adamantly rejected his mother's suggestion that he had imagined the presence. Actually, Mrs. McDonald wasn't so sure herself that the intruder was purely imaginery, but she wasn't about to let Peter know that. Nevertheless, hoping to make Peter feel better, she ordered the "man" to leave.

"Suddenly everything was normal again," she later wrote. "The atmosphere changed dramatically—it was warm again."

Peter went back to sleep and all was quiet the rest of the night. Still uneasy about what had happened, the next morning Mrs. McDonald checked outside the window to see what could have caused the scratching Peter had reported. She couldn't find anything, which did nothing to ease her fears. But she comforted herself with the thought that at least whatever had caused the strange incident was gone, and the incident was over. Still, she couldn't get it out of her mind.

It was on her mind when she went to bed that night. And at 2:00 A.M., when she heard Peter's terrified little voice calling her name, she expected the worst—and she found it: the same inexplicable coldness, the same insistence on Peter's part that an evil man was staring at him.

The scene repeated itself every night for the next few weeks. "Eventually," Mrs. McDonald recalled, "I became accustomed to that incredible, shocking coldness that met me at the doorway to Peter's room. It was more than the chill one feels when frightened. It was almost like a force of hate."

One thing changed, though. Now the man was smiling, with a terrifying evil leer, as if he were waiting for something.

"PLEASE, I DON'T WANT TO GO!"

Mrs. McDonald could never see the man, but she sensed his eyes on her. She grew to loathe him. She felt he was laughing at her. Yet she had some strange power over him. When she would order him to leave, he would.

As the frightening visitations continued, Peter claimed he could see the man more clearly. He had, the boy said, "red hair and a mustache." An aura of arrogance, impatience, and growing anger emanated from him. He always stood in one corner, away from Peter's brother, who strangely enough always slept through the episodes.

Now Peter was saying that the man had taken to waving his arms, as if beckoning to the boy to come away with him. Peter would shriek, "Please, Mama, I don't want to go!"

Then the man began to speak to Peter, expressing explicitly and commandingly his desire to have the lad accompany him. His visitations were longer, and he was becoming harder and harder to get rid of.

One morning, after a particularly horrifying encounter, Mrs. McDonald was doing her daily chores while Peter played alone in his room. Suddenly the boy appeared. He had a peculiar lazy grin on his face. He approached his mother, threw his arms around her and said, "Oh, Mama, I love you." Then he seemed to stagger. Something was wrong. Peter was intoxicated!

As she followed him to his room, she passed the bathroom. Looking inside, she immediately saw what had happened. Her son had taken a chair, reached into the medicine cabinet and swallowed 36 aspirins. By the time Mrs. McDonald got Peter to the West Hudson Hospital in Kearny, New Jersey, his system had absorbed the pills, and it was no longer possible to pump them out of his stomach.

For two days Peter hovered between life and death. His situation was further imperiled by his already-weak heart. But his doctors worked valiantly to save him. A few days later he came home, weak but very much alive.

At 2:00 A.M. that night the evil man returned. When his mother entered his room, feeling as usual the hideous, hate-filled coldness, Peter told her the man was no longer in the corner he had always occupied; now he was "on a horse" on the other side of the room, where Peter's brother lay sleeping. The man's face was twisted in anger, and he was shaking his fist. Then he jerked the reins, and he and the horse rode off!

"For the first time since it began," Mrs. McDonald wrote nine years later, "I felt as if, finally, it was over—really over. The fear was gone. The cold was

gone. I cradled Peter in my arms and told my little
son that I 'knew' the man would never come back.

"So far he has not returned."

THE BEDROOM INVADERS

The events Martha McDonald has recounted are an
especially frightening example of a class of phenomena John A. Keel, a veteran investigator of
paranormal phenomena, has called "bedroom invaders." One of the most famous persons to experience the phenomena was Sir Arthur Conan Doyle,
creator of the Sherlock Holmes series and an ardent
Spiritualist, who recorded the following in his 1910
book *The Edge of the Unknown*:

> It was in my bedroom in Crowborough. I
> awakened in the night with the clear con-
> sciousness that there was someone in the
> room and that the presence was not of this
> world. I was lying with my back to the room,
> acutely awake, but utterly unable to move. It
> was physically impossible for me to turn my
> body and face this visitor. I heard measured
> steps across the room. I was conscious (with-
> out seeing it) that someone was bending over
> me, and then I heard a voice saying in a loud
> whisper, 'Doyle, I come to tell you that I am
> sorry.' A minute later my disability disap-
> peared, and I was able to turn, but all was
> black darkness and perfectly still. My wife
> had not awakened, and knew nothing of
> what had passed.

From his own investigations, John Keel learned just how common these kinds of incidents are. He writes in *Strange Creatures From Time and Space* (1970), "In the past three years, we have published two popular magazine articles on these bedroom invaders, and we were amazed by the amount of mail these pieces drew. Many readers wrote to tell us, sometimes in absorbing detail, of their own experiences with this uncanny phenomenon."

In one case a Maine woman reported that one night she had been awakened by a slap on the face. Opening her eyes, she was startled to see dark figures grouped around her bed and staring at her. One night in May 1968, a young man staying as a guest in a house in Superior, Wisconsin, observed a huge shape at the foot of his bed. It had, he said, "a massive head with huge broad shoulders ... It moved from the right side of the bed to the left and then disappeared."

Individuals interested in esoteric subjects, whether the occult, paranormal or even ufological, sometimes report being harassed by strange, apparitional figures or by odd-looking "people" dressed in dark clothing. At the same time they may suffer other kinds of problems, such as abruptly declining health, nervous exhaustion, and crippling anxiety.

A PLAGUE OF ANGELS

One researcher into the esoteric has recorded what happened to him as he was compiling a comprehensive work entitled *Dictionary of Angels*, published in 1967. Gustav Davidson writes in the introduction:

> At this stage of the quest, I was literally bedeviled by angels. They stalked and leaguered me, by night and day. I could not tell the evil from the good ... I moved, indeed, in a twilight zone of tall presences ... I remember one occasion—it was winter and getting dark—returning home from a neighboring farm. I had cut across an unfamiliar field. Suddenly a nightmarish shape loomed up in front of me, barring my progress. After a paralyzing moment, I managed to fight my way past the phantom. The next morning I could not be sure whether I had encountered a ghost, an angel, a demon, or God. There were other such moments and other such encounters, when I passed from terror to trance, from intimations of realms unguessed at to the uneasy conviction that, beyond the reach of our senses, beyond the arch of all our experience sacred and profane, there was only—to use an expression of Paul's in Timothy 4—"fable and endless genealogy."

Dabblers in "occult toys" such as Ouija boards and planchettes sometimes complain that the disembodied entities with which they believe they are communicating will not let them alone, even when they are not using the boards. The entities may try to possess them or in other ways attempt to influence their conduct. They may take up residence in the individuals' residences and manifest as apparitions, poltergeists, or psychic vampires, draining physical and spiritual energy from their victims. Of course such things may well have a psychological explanation. But whether they are psychological or paranormal in origin, we do know that Ouija boards and other such devices can call up destructive energies, especially when operated by occult novices who have no real idea of what they are doing.

But there are times when even those skilled in occult practice and keenly aware of its dangers can fall victim to paranormal assault, as the following story dramatically demonstrates.

ONE NIGHT IN ENGLAND

The noted occult writer, Melita Denning, has recounted one of the oddest psychic attack accounts ever recorded.

It began late one evening in 1975, when a small group of people emerged from a lecture delivered at London's College of Psychic Science and meandered up Victoria Street on their way to a restaurant to continue their conversations before turning in.

Two of them, publisher Fletcher Garland and psychic Kitty Somerset, walked slightly behind the rest and talked quietly but intently about matters of mutual interest. But then Somerset lapsed into silence and when she failed to answer a question,

Garland looked at her anxiously, wondering if something was wrong. In the dim light he saw her suddenly remove her shoes. The next thing he knew, she had stepped into the street. She seemed in a dazed state, as if lost in a trance.

Other members of the group, noting the abrupt silence, turned and were horrified to see a speeding car narrowly miss Somerset. Garland dashed into the street and had almost reached her when Somerset fell violently forward "as if poleaxed," in Garland's words. She crashed hard into the concrete and lay still. Another car passed by, this one so close that it ran over her outstretched blond hair.

As Garland waved oncoming cars away, the others helped Somerset to her feet. Even though it was obvious she was badly hurt, and in a state of shock, she insisted that they continue on to the restaurant. She said she would feel better there. Besides, she wanted to phone someone.

But on their arrival at the cafe, Somerset was overcome with pain, and it was clear to all concerned that she had to be taken to the nearest hospital as soon as possible. Fletcher and Roberta Livingstone, another member of the group, called a taxi and rode with Somerset to the emergency ward.

Asked how she had become injured, her two friends could only tell doctors that she had been "in a road accident," and fallen down. But her injuries were so extensive that no simple fall was adequate to explain them. Her neck, collarbone, wrist, and three ribs on her right side (the side on which she had fallen) were fractured; the fingers of her right hand were so violently dislocated that they were lying against the back of her hand. If her friends had not known better, they would have thought she had fallen from some great height.

At first the doctors thought she might have suffered an epileptic fit, but Somerset had no history of such an affliction. Nor did she have abnormally brittle bones. Although much about the incident baffled them, the doctors knew that if they did not operate on her neck, she would be paralyzed from the pressure on the spinal cord.

A few days later, as she lay in bed slowly recovering, Somerset made a phone call. She asked the man who answered the phone if she could speak to Ralph Seigel.

OCCULT TRAGEDY

Ralph Seigel, 10 years Somerset's junior, was an odd, unprepossessing man who some months earlier had come to see Somerset seeking psychic guidance. He told her he hoped to master occultism and was reading extensively on the subject. He was even working as a watchman so that he would have long, peaceful hours in which to continue his studies.

Somerset cautiously took him on as an occasional pupil, but kept herself aloof from him, not wanting to encourage him in a romantic way. She was a beautiful former model who naturally attracted men, but she was not attracted to this peculiarly passive, yet obsessive fellow. She tried to space their visits as much as possible.

Nonetheless, he began to confide in her more and more. He told her he was beginning to learn how to project his astral body. But he also told her about his past, about a bizarre and pathetic relationship he had had with a woman for whom he had worked as a domestic servant. The woman, a wealthy widow, had taken him as a lover, but had quickly transformed the relationship into a sadomasochistic exercise. She had treated him as a slave, beaten and otherwise abused him. He had accepted this and adored her. Then, after a brief illness she died, leaving him desperately sad and lonely.

As he related the story, Somerset realized that her aloof, distant manner, far from discouraging the young man, had actually drawn him to her, reminding him of the woman he had loved and lost. Not wanting to hurt him, but still desiring to remove herself from a potentially unpleasant situation, she further reduced the frequency of their meetings.

The night she had her accident, she realized it had been nearly two months since she last had seen him. She vowed to call him immediately to make amends but was unable to do so until she had spent some time recovering in the hospital.

When she finally did make her call, a night watchman whose voice she did not recognize answered. She asked to speak to Ralph Seigel. The man replied, "Didn't you hear of his death?"

It developed that he had committed suicide at work two weeks earlier. Somerset learned that he had stabbed himself with a pair of scissors at the same moment she had suffered her terrible fall.

As she lay back stunned and strickened, she remembered something Seigel had said in one of their last conversations. He said he could project astrally and visit people, but there was one problem: he would get so excited that he would "bump into them." But could the undersized body of the young occultist have been magnified enough in its psychic state to have caused such a catastrophic accident?

Somerset thought of these words from Aleister Crowley's *Magick in Theory and Practice:*

> The practical details of the Bloody Sacrifice may be studied in various ethnological manuals ... The method of killing is practically uniform. The animal should be stabbed to the heart ... The victim must ... also not be too large, the amount of energy disengaged is almost unimaginably great, and out of all anticipated proportion to the strength of the animal. Consequently, the magician may easily be overwhelmed ... by the force which he has let loose.

HOW DO YOU KNOW YOU'RE BEING ATTACKED?

How do you know when you are under psychic attack?

First, a word or two of common sense: Don't jump to conclusions. If you find yourself having problems, being plagued by bad dreams or suffering from illness without immediate apparent cause, first investigate the normal world of your five senses for the explanation. Chances are, that's where you'll find it.

Some people who think they are being attacked psychically are mentally ill. They may hear voices tormenting them or commanding them to commit antisocial acts. They may suffer from hallucinations of persons or entities that they think are assaulting their psyches.

A person so deeply schizophrenic should not be encouraged in his delusions, of course. And most of the time it does not take a trained psychiatrist to recognize the symptoms. Mental illness this advanced so impairs an individual's ability to function in society that he may not even be able to conduct a rational conversation.

We are concerned here with normal, sane people who reported extraordinary experiences. Extraordinary experiences of the paranormal kind are far from rare; according to all evidence from polls and surveys on the subject, most of us will at some point in our lives experience such an event, whether it involves ESP, an encounter with an apparition, a sensation of separation from the body, a memory of what seems to be a previous life, mind over matter—or psychic attack.

From his own survey of the "hag" experience, as we have already noted, behavioral psychologist David Hufford came to believe that a variety of psychic attack occurs to one person in every six, or 15 percent of the population. Hufford also found that psychological disturbance played no part in such reports. The great majority of individuals who claimed such things had happened to them were quite sane. He concluded that such events could be explained only in part by conventional means. In his book on the subject, he left open the possibility that some paranormal agency might be involved.

SYMPTOMS

As Dion Fortune observes in her famous book *Psychic Self-Defense*, there are many kinds of psychic attacks. Generally speaking, however, we can state with some degree of certainty that one is taking place if the following symptoms are observed:

(1) The victim feels a crushing weight upon his chest and a sense of fear and paranoia.
(2) As the attack continues over days, weeks, or months, the victim is afflicted

with nervous exhaustion. With that may come a physical deterioration.

(3) Upon awakening, the victim discovers bruises which cannot be accounted for by any conscious waking experience. The bruises may have a definite pattern, depicting a form with some symbolic significance suggestive, for example, of evil.

(4) Foul odors inexplicably appear. Strange footprints starting suddenly and ending just as abruptly are observed. Odd sounds and poltergeist manifestations occur.

Again, mundane causes may still be responsible, and the victim should not abandon the search for a "reasonable" explanation. But at some point even the most rational person may have to open his mind to the possibility that extraordinary forces are causing his troubles, if these kinds of strange events continue to occur.

What are these extraordinary forces?

MALEVOLENT PSYCHOSIS

A number of different paranormal forces figure in psychic attacks, as we have seen from some of the incidents we have reviewed. The first of these is psychokinesis (PK), known popularly as "mind over matter." PK is a mental phenomenon. It is harbored in the unconscious. Some gifted people seem to be able to use it more or less at will to perform assorted harmless stunts, from bending spoons to influencing subatomic particles. Others, most prominently healers, use it for beneficial ends such as the curing of organic illnesses.

But PK also has a destructive side. Parapsychologists believe that many poltergeist episodes, in which an invisible presence goes on a rampage through a house, harassing its occupants and smashing furniture and other valuables, are caused not by spirits, but by the unconscious unleashing of PK by a psychologically troubled individual. In a sense the individual's inner turmoil is played out in dramatic fashion in the outside world.

If the "poltergeist agent" consciously means no harm, the same cannot be said of those who intentionally direct PK against persons they wish to hurt. They do this by focusing on a mental or physical image of the intended victim. In the former case this is usually just a vivid recollection of what the person looks like; in the latter it may be a doll, a photograph, or a drawing representing the victim, or even some item belonging to him (anything from a strand of hair to an item of property).

It should be noted that the person plotting the evil deed may never have heard of "psychokinesis," a word most likely to be known by intellectuals familiar with the technical literature of parapsychology. He may think he is calling up demons or other malevolent entities, when in fact the paranormal force being drawn upon is from his own heart of darkness.

ATTACK IN THE ASTRAL

For most persons the experience of astral projection is involuntary and unexpected. They may suddenly find their "selves" separated from their bodies and have no idea how such a thing could have happened; nor will they exercise any control over how long they are out of their bodies, where they want to go or what they want to do in their "soul bodies."

Some persons, however, are either innately capable of projecting at will or have mastered the techniques that make it possible. (These techniques are described in *The Llewellyn Practical Guide to Astral Projection* by Melita Denning and Osborne Phillips.) Among these, a few use their astral bodies as vehicles to attack someone they don't like.

Interestingly enough, some experts on the subject of vampires believe that this is what vampirism really is. There is no reason to attribute vampire attacks to the physical likes of Count Dracula and his kith and kin, who are products purely of the imagination. There is evidence that real victims of vampires are set upon by a malevolent astral form.

A truly horrifying instance was recorded by the Asian explorer Ethelbert Forbes Skertchley who described the phenomenon in an article published in an 1896 issue of *The Journal of the Asiatic Society of Bengal*. A Filipino tribe living on the island of Cagayan Sulu, on the far southwest tip of the Philippines, lived in fear, Skertchley wrote, of a people called the Berbalangs, who lived by themselves in a small village at the center of the island.

The Berbalangs were cannibals who periodically robbed graves and ate the entrails of recently deceased people. But the island's small population limited the supply of human flesh. Therefore, Skertchley wrote:

> When they feel the craving for a feed of human flesh, they go away into the grass, and having carefully hidden their bodies, hold their breath and fall into a trance. Their astral bodies are liberated in the form of heads with the feet attached to the ears as wings. They fly away, and entering a house make their way into the body of one of the occupants and feed on his entrails, when of course he dies in fearful agony.
>
> The Berbalangs may be heard coming, as they make a moaning noise which is loud at a distance and dies away to a feeble wail as they approach. When they are near you the sound of their wings may be heard, and the flashing lights of their eyes can be seen like dancing fireflies in the dark.

FLIGHT OF THE VAMPIRES

During his stay with the Cagayans, Skertchley heard so much about the Berbalangs from so many different informants, that despite an understandable skepticism about "primitive superstition" he could no longer hide his curiosity. He asked if he could see the Berbalangs. The natives cringed in fear at the very idea, but at last one of them, a young man named Matali, agreed to take him there.

But when they got within sight of the village, Matali refused to go any further, so Skertchley walked the remaining half-mile by himself. Once there, he was surprised to find the place entirely deserted. He entered several of the huts and found freshly prepared food on the tables, as if the occupants had been about to eat their evening meals when something had suddenly called them away.

I returned to Matali, Skertchley wrote:

> And on telling him of the deserted state of the village, he turned pale and implored me to come back at once as the Berbalangs were out and it would be dangerous to return in the dark.
>
> The sun was setting as we started on our homeward way. Before we had covered half the distance, it was quite dark. There was not a breath of air stirring. We were in the middle of an open valley with no trees, when we heard a loud moaning noise like someone in pain. Matali immediately crouched down in the long grass and pulled me down beside him: he said the Berbalangs were coming down the valley and our only chance was that they might pass us by without seeing us. We lay hidden there while the moaning

sound grew fainter, and Matali whispered that they were coming nearer.

Presently the sound died away to a faint wail and the sound of wings became audible, while a lot of little dancing lights, like fireflies only reddish, passed over us. I could feel Matali's grip tighten on my arm and I felt a nasty creepy sensation about the roots of my hair, but after the lights had passed, the noise of the wings ceased, the moaning grew louder, and Matali told me they had gone by and for the time being we were safe.

We continued on our way down the valley, and on passing an isolated house at some distance from the path, the moaning grew faint again, and Matali said the Berbalangs had certainly gone into the house, and he trusted that Hassan, the owner, had a coconut pearl to protect him." The Cagayans believed that coconut pearls were a magical charm which could drive off astral Berbalangs.

Now I knew Hassan, to whose house the Berbalangs had gone, and decided to call on him the next day and see what account he had to give of the night's occurrences.

Accordingly, shortly after daybreak, I started off alone, as I could get no one to accompany me, and in due course came to Hassan's house. There was no sign of anyone about, so I tried the door but found it fastened. I shouted several times but no one answered, so, putting my shoulder to the door, I gave a good push and it fell in. I entered the house and looked round but could see no one; going further in I suddenly started back, for, huddled up on the bed, with hands clenched, face distorted, and eyes staring as if in horror, lay my friend Hassan—dead.

I have stated about the facts just as they occurred, and am quite unable to give any explanation of them.

EVIL ELEMENTALS

Elementals, or elementary beings, are earth-based spirits of widely varying levels of moral development. An unscrupulous practitioner of magic who knows how to manipulate them can use them as vehicles for psychic attack.

In *The Astral Plane*, C.W. Leadbeater tells how it is done:

A feeling of envious or jealous hatred towards another person sends an evil elemental to hover over him and seek for a weak point through which it can operate; and if the feeling be persistent, such a creature may be continually nourished by it and thereby be enabled to protract its undesirable activity for a long period. It can, however, produce no effect upon the person towards whom it is directed unless he has himself some tendency which it can foster—some fulcrum for its lever, so to speak. From the aura of a man of pure thought and good life all such influ-

ences at once rebound, finding nothing upon
which they can fasten ...

It is not only the practiced magician who can
cause this sort of psychic infestation. The magician knows exactly what he is doing. But the same
elemental forces can be triggered into operation
by an ordinary person who bears an overwhelming hatred of someone else and who fervently
wishes that other person ill.

There are also evil elementals which prey on people for their own malevolent purposes. Dion Fortune
thinks that these beings "probably originated
through the workings of Black Magic, which took
the essential evil essence and organized it for purposes of its own." They cause nightmares, terrifying
hallucinations, cold sensations, loud noises, foul
smells, manifestations of slime and blood, and other
unpleasant phenomena. The evil "man" who tried to
kill little Peter McDonald apparently was one of
these entities.

In a sense these evil elementals are psychic vul-
tures. They are drawn to the "scent" of evil. For
example, they will be attracted to any kind of malevolent operation at work on the astral plane,
thereby magnifying the amount of harm wrought
on a victim. There is no situation that an evil elemental will not delight in making worse.

THE DANGEROUS DEAD

In 1978 an American psychiatrist and speaker known as Allison discussed a visualization technique that involves a patient directing angry feelings into a bottle. In his clinical work, Allison had found that this technique was often effective in loosening the grip of the alter-personality over the primary personality. However, one time, even though he and his nurse had worked with the technique for over two hours, a patient's alter-personality remained firmly in control.

Allison and his associate felt strangely drained. The nurse had an intense headache, and the psychiatrist was so weak that he barely managed to drive home without passing out at the wheel. As soon as he entered his house, he collapsed into bed. In the middle of the night he was awakened by agonizing stomach pains. He got to the bathroom, where he discovered he was bleeding from both ends of his gastro-intestinal tract. He then lapsed into unconsciousness. When his wife found him on the bathroom floor, she called an ambulance.

Allison spent 11 days in the hospital before he was well enough to return to work. Once there, he saw his patient, Helen, again. "When I questioned the patient," he reported, "I found that the entity that I had presumed was an alter-personality claimed to be the spirit of a witch who had died in England in 1890. She claimed to be possessing this patient, and I had angered her, so she struck back at me."

In his book *Minds in Many Pieces*, Allison recounts similarly dramatic cases in which he or persons close to a multiple personality sufferer fell victim to psychic attack by alter-personalities claiming to be spirits. Allison believes it is possible that some of them are victims of this kind of attack. He feels that an individual going through the terrible problems associated with a multiple personality disorder is vulnerable to possession by evil spirits who take up "residence" along with the imaginary personalities.

He is not the first investigator to come to such a conclusion. In the early twentieth century, James Hyslop, one of the early pioneers of psychical research, came to believe that some cases of mental illness are caused by spirit obsession or possession. Dr. Titus Bull, a prominent New York physician and associate of Hyslop's, would take patients who had not responded to more conventional therapy to mediums. Bull would contact the invading spirits and force them to leave. He claimed considerable success with this unorthodox treatment.

Dr. Carl Wickland would treat mental patients with a static electric shock, which he thought forced the possessing spirits to leave, at least temporarily, and enter his wife, a gifted medium. The physician would then talk with the spirits and persuade them to let his patient alone. He, too, claimed the technique worked. He described his work in a famous book called *Thirty Years Among the Dead*.

EVIL FROM BEYOND THE GRAVE

Thousands of Grade-Z horror movies and hack novels with occult themes—not to mention thousands of years of superstitious beliefs—have caused most human beings to think of the dead as a threat to the living and ghosts as entities up to no good. The evidence from human experience, documented in the serious literature of psychical research, shows us otherwise, however. While contacts between the dead and the living are in fact not at all uncommon (as any number of polls and surveys have shown), the experiences are positive in the great majority of cases. Usually they involve the return of a deceased spouse, relative, or friend, and they provide a measure of comfort to the grief-stricken living.

But it is not only good people who die and survive. There are deranged people who die but who remain, even as spirits, evil. Sometimes, if the conclusions of Allison, Wickland, Hyslop, Bull, and others are correct, they prey on the mentally ill whose "psychic shields" are down. They may also attack normal people who happen to be in the wrong place at the wrong time.

Evil spirits may also come from those who were not bad people, but who led desperately unhappy lives, or who died terrible deaths. Their spirits have been affected adversely—in other words, by the circumstances of their lives or deaths. It is even possible that these spirits are not consciously evil, but simply confused, desperate, and not fully aware of the consequences of their actions. But they can still be dangerous to the living.

Malevolent discarnates are usually associated with haunted houses, of course, but they are certainly not limited to such places. They have been known to occupy other geographical locations, such as a stretch of highway (where they may cause deadly accidents), a swamp, a factory, or in fact, just about any place one can imagine. Typically the discarnate is associated with the place in some way; he may have died there, perhaps, or committed some monstrous act.

We also know that at least some evil spirits are not bound to any particular place and can follow their victims to the ends of the earth if they so desire.

PSYCHIC SELF-DEFENSE

What is your chance of being psychically attacked at some point in your life?

It is fairly high, the evidence suggests. That does not necessarily mean that you will be victimized in a dramatic, life-threatening way, but it is distinctly possible that at some time or another you will incur the wrath of someone whose anger at you will find paranormal expression, whether your attacker realizes it or not. (If he does realize it and knows exactly what he is doing, you could be in for a very harrowing time.) But fierce, concentrated anger can trigger malevolent psychokinesis or bring an evil elemental into the picture, even if the human agent doesn't know that such things are possible.

Ours is an intensely stressful, violent, competitive age. There is much negative energy polluting our psychic environment, and growing numbers of people are turning to the occult. Most of them, fortunately, are doing it with the best of motives—to enhance their own spiritual development and to play their own small parts in the evolutionary betterment of the human race. As in any human endeavor, however, there are those who use their powers for destructive ends. The occasional press accounts of ritual killings of people and animals represent only the tip of the iceberg. Much of the negative occultism is not occurring on a physical level. In a society that officially rejects the "psychic" as superstitious foolishness, practitioners of occult evil have virtually free rein to prey on helpless persons who have no idea how to protect themselves.

You can protect yourself, however. Anybody can master the techniques, which are explained clearly in *The Llewellyn Practical Guide to Psychic Self-Defense and Well-Being* by Melita Denning and Osborne Phillips. Denning and Phillips show you not only how to protect yourself from the negative psychic energies that bombard us, but how to employ your own positive energies to gain control of your life and bring yourself to vitality, health, confidence, decisiveness, and spiritual awareness. It's a book, in other words, for *anyone* who seeks to triumph over adverse circumstances of all kinds and to establish contact with the Higher Self, the source of all psychic well-being.

As the authors put it:

> Psychic self-defense concerns YOU. It merits the attention of every intelligent human being. It has a vital part to fulfill: in our duty towards ourselves, in our responsibility towards our dear ones and towards all who may be in our care, and in our responsibility to society and to the biosphere as a whole. Psychic self-defense is important in our physical and emotional, even in our mental and spiritual well-being ...

The key to psychic self-defense is in knowing how to strengthen your aura, enough to make it invulnerable to negative forces, however powerful. This is not an ability we are born with; it must be learned. The techniques are known to experienced occultists, and they are not terribly difficult to master if one is willing to practice them regularly. Denning and Phillips outline, in clear, easy-to-understand prose, the daily exercises you can practice to strengthen your psychic muscles. Freedom from the fear of outside aggression and manipulation can liberate your life. And this kind of spiritual freedom is available to you, if you know how to claim it. *The Llewellyn Practical Guide to Psychic Self-*

Defense and Well-Being shows you how to find what was yours all along: life, strength, happiness.

Most of all, remember: You don't have to be a victim. You have the power. It is in your aura. All you have to do is to recognize and tap it. You will be astonished at what happens to you. You will be able to draw on two worlds: the material world and the spiritual world—and you will never be the same again. Protection from psychic attack is merely the first step on the path to new worlds of adventure and enlightenment. Are you ready for the journey?

While psychic self-defense is just one element of a total program of *psychic well-being* that involves daily exercises to channel spiritual energies and strengthen your aura, there is no reason that you should remain without psychic protection … *starting right now!*

Take an object that you can wear or keep with you at all times. A ring or wrist watch will do, but a bracelet, necklace, or waist-chain is better. Clean the chosen object in some way: the feeling that it is *really clean* should culminate what you've done. Seat yourself comfortably, preferably with your back straight, your feet together, and the chosen object held loosely in your strongest hand.

Close your eyes and physically relax your body. Breathe slowly and evenly. With each in-breath feel a flow of energy rise from your feet to the top of your head, and with each out-breath feel that energy flow from the top of your head to your feet. Feel yourself calmly growing in strength as the energy flows through your body. After ten or more breaths, when you feel strong and alert, visualize a sphere of pure white light just above your head and *know* that this is your own Highest Self—free of all fear and pain, pure in the Divine Force that is everywhere.

Visualize that sphere forming an egg-shape of intense blue light all around you, and *know* that this is your psychic shield that will protect you from harm as it grows in strength. Continue breathing gently and evenly, feeling the strength in your body while holding this image.

Grasp the chosen object tightly in your hand, and feel that strength suddenly surge into your hand and into the object. Hold that object, hold that feeling, and hold the image of your psychic shield all around you. Project that fully charged battery, constantly energizing your psychic shield. *You are protected!*

But *psychic well-being* depends on a daily program as described in Denning and Phillips' book. Start that as soon as possible so that you grow in strength and spiritual resources.

On the following pages you will find listed, with their current prices, some of the books now available on related subjects. Your book dealer stocks most of these and will stock new titles in the Llewellyn series as they become available. We urge your patronage.

TO GET A FREE CATALOG

To obtain our full catalog, you are invited to write (see address below) for our bi-monthly news magazine/catalog, *Llewellyn's New Worlds of Mind and Spirit*. A sample copy is free, and will continue coming to you at no cost as long as you are an active mail customer. Or you may subscribe for just $10 in the USA and Canada ($20 overseas, first class mail). Many bookstores also have *New Worlds* available to their customers. Ask for it.

TO ORDER BOOKS AND TAPES

If your book store does not carry the titles described on the following pages, you may order them directly from Llewellyn by sending the full price in U.S. funds, plus postage and handling (see below).

Credit card orders: VISA, MasterCard, American Express are accepted. Call us toll-free within the United States and Canada at 1-800-THE-MOON.

Postage and Handling: Include $4 postage and handling for orders $15 and under; $5 for orders *over* $15. There are no postage and handling charges for orders over $100. Postage and handling rates are subject to change. We ship UPS whenever possible within the continental United States; delivery is guaranteed. Please provide your street address as UPS does not deliver to P.O. boxes. Orders shipped to Alaska, Hawaii, Canada, Mexico and Puerto Rico will be sent via first class mail. Allow 4-6 weeks for delivery. **International orders:** Airmail – add retail price of each book and $5 for each non-book item (audiotapes, etc.); Surface mail – add $1 per item.

Minnesota residents please add 7% sales tax.

Llewellyn Worldwide
P.O. Box 64383 L352, St. Paul, MN 55164-0383, U.S.A.

For customer service, call (612) 291-1970.

THE LLEWELLYN PRACTICAL GUIDE TO PSYCHIC SELF-DEFENSE AND WELL-BEING
by Denning & Phillips

Psychic well-being and psychic self-defense are two sides of the same coin, just as are physical health and resistance to disease. Each person (and every living thing) is surrounded by an electromagnetic force field, or AURA, that can provide the means to psychic self-defense and to dynamic well-being. This book explores the world of very real "psychic warfare" of which we are all victims.

Every person in our modern world is subjected to psychic stress and psychological bombardment: advertising promotions that play upon primitive emotions, political and religious appeals that work on feelings of insecurity and guilt, noise, threats of violence and war, news of crime and disaster, etc.

This book shows the nature of genuine psychic attacks—ranging from actual acts of black magic to bitter jealousy and hate—and the reality of psychic stress, the structure of the psyche and its interrelationship with the physical body. It shows how each person must develop his weakened aura into a powerful defense-shield, thereby gaining both physical protection and energetic well-being that can extend to protection from physical violence, accidents ... even ill health.

0-87542-190-3, 306 pgs., 5-¼ x 8, illus., softcover $9.95

THE LLEWELLYN PRACTICAL GUIDE TO
THE DEVELOPMENT OF PSYCHIC POWERS
by Denning & Phillips

You may not realize it, but you already have the ability to use ESP, Astral Vision and Clairvoyance, Divination, Dowsing, Prophecy, and Communication with Spirits.

Written by two of the most knowledgeable experts in the world of psychic development, this book is a complete course—teaching you, step-by-step, how to develop these powers that actually have been yours since birth. Using the techniques, you will soon be able to move objects at a distance, see into the future, know the thoughts and feelings of another person, find lost objects and locate water using your formerly latent talents.

Psychic powers are as much a natural ability as any other talent. You'll learn to play with these new skills, working with groups of friends to accomplish things you never would have believed possible before reading this book. The text shows you how to make the equipment you can use, the exercises you can do—many of them at any time, anywhere—and how to use your abilities to change your life and the lives of those close to you. Many of the exercises are presented in forms that can be adapted as games for pleasure and fun, as well as development.

0-87542-191-1, 272 pgs., 5-¼ x 8, illus., softcover $9.95

PSYCHIC EMPOWERMENT
A Seven-Day Plan for Self-Development
Joe Slate, Ph.D.

Use 100% of your mind power in just one week! You've heard it before: each of us is filled with an abundance of untapped power—yet we only use *one-tenth* of its potential. Now a clinical psychologist and famed researcher in parapsychology shows you *how* to probe your mind's psychic faculties and manifest your capacity to *access* the higher planes of the mind.

The psychic experience validates your true nature and connects you to your inner knowing. Dr. Slate reveals the life-changing nature of psychic phenomena—including telepathy, out-of-body experiences and automatic writing. At the same time, he shows you how to develop a host of psychic abilities including psychokinesis, crystal gazing, and table tilting.

The final section of the book outlines his accelerated Seven-Day Psychic Development Plan through which you can unleash your innate power and wisdom without further delay.

1-56718-635-1, 6 x 9, 256 pp., softbound $12.95

HOW TO DEVELOP & USE PSYCHOMETRY
Ted Andrews

What if a chair could speak? What if you could pick up a pen and tell what kind of day its owner had had? What if you could touch someone and know what kind of person he or she truly was—or sense pain or illness? These examples just scratch the surface of the applications of psychometry: the ability to read the psychic imprints that exist upon objects, people and places.

Everyone is psychic. Unfortunately, most of the time we brush aside our psychic impressions. Now, everyone can learn to develop their own natural sensitivities. *How to Develop and Use Psychometry* will teach you to assess your own abilities and provide you with a step-by-step process for developing your natural psychic abilities, including over twenty-five exercises to heighten your normal sense of touch to new levels of sensitivity.

With a little awareness and practice, you can learn to use your inborn intuitive abilities to read the history of objects and places ... locate missing or lost articles ... develop intimacy ... even find missing persons. *How to Develop and Use Psychometry* gives you all of the techniques you need to effectively "touch" the natural psychic within yourself!

1-56718-025-6, mass market, 224 pp., illus. **$3.99**

HOW TO MEET & WORK WITH SPIRIT GUIDES
by Ted Andrews

We often experience spirit contact in our lives but fail to recognize it for what it is. Now you can learn to access and attune to beings such as guardian angels, nature spirits and elementals, spirit totems, archangels, gods and goddesses—as well as family and friends after their physical death.

Contact with higher soul energies strengthens the will and enlightens the mind. Through a series of simple exercises, you can safely and gradually increase your awareness of spirits and your ability to identify them. You will learn to develop an intentional and directed contact with any number of spirit beings. Discover meditations to open up your subconscious. Learn which acupressure points effectively stimulate your intuitive faculties. Find out how to form a group for spirit work, use crystal balls, perform automatic writing, attune your aura for spirit contact, use sigils to contact the great archangels and much more! Read *How to Meet and Work with Spirit Guides* and take your first steps through the corridors of life beyond the physical.

0–87542–008–7, 192 pgs., mass market, illus. $4.99

PSYCHIC POWER
Techniques & Inexpensive Devices
that Increase Your Psychic Powers
by Charles Cosimano

Although popular in many parts of the world, Radionics machines have had little application in America, UNTIL NOW! *Psychic Power* introduces these machines to America with a new purpose: to increase your psychic powers!

Using the easy, step-by-step instructions, and for less than a $10 investment, you can build a machine which will allow you to read other people's minds, influence their thoughts, communicate with their dreams and be more successful when you do divinations such as working with Tarot cards or pendulums.

For thousands of years, people have looked for an easy, simple and sure way to increase their psychic abilities. Now, the science of psionics allows you to do just that! This book is practical, fun and an excellent source for those wishing to achieve results with etheric energies.

If you just want a book to read, you will find this a wonderful title to excitingly fill a few hours. But if you can spare a few minutes to actually build and use these devices, you will be able to astound yourself and your friends. We are not talking about guessing which numbers will come up on a pair of dice at a mark slightly above average. With practice, you will be able to choose which numbers will come up more often than not! But don't take our word for it. Read the book, build the devices and find out for yourself.

0-87542-097-4, 224 pgs., mass market, illus. $3.95

THE PSYCHIC SIDE OF DREAMS
by Hans Holzer

Wakefulness and the dream state go hand in hand, equal partners in our day-to-day existence, sharing consciousness, and forming and two halves of our lives. *The Psychic Side of Dreams* (newly reprinted with added material) acquaints readers with the true nature of the dream state, the many aspects of dreaming, and how to open the dream channel so wide that it serves as a secondary (or superior) world of perception.

Illustrated with numerous case histories from people around the world, *The Psychic Side of Dreams* explains the different types of dreams: anxiety dreams, out-of-body experiences ("falling dreams"), nightmares, prophetic dreams (in which future events are foreseen or foretold), warning dreams (in which future events are depicted so that we can alter the results), survival dreams (including communication with the world beyond or with the dead), ESP dreams (psychic dreams that relate to events taking place at exactly the same moment), reincarnation dreams and recurrent dreams.

Everyone dreams, everyone can learn to interpret dreams, and we can all use dreams to expand knowledge and control of our lives. Hans Holzer's objective and documented investigation will show you how you can, too.

0-87542-369-8, 288 pgs., mass market, softcover $4.95

THE SECRET OF LETTING GO
by Guy Finley

Whether you need to let go of a painful heartache, a destructive habit, a frightening worry or a nagging discontent, *The Secret of Letting Go* shows you how to call upon your own hidden powers and how they can take you through and beyond any challenge or problem. This book reveals the secret source of a brand-new kind of inner strength.

In the light of your new and higher self-understanding, emotional difficulties such as loneliness, fear, anxiety and frustration fade into nothingness as you happily discover they never really existed in the first place.

With a foreword by Desi Arnaz Jr., and introduction by Dr. Jesse Freeland, *The Secret of Letting Go* is a pleasing balance of questions and answers, illustrative examples, truth tales, and stimulating dialogues that allow the reader to share in the exciting discoveries that lead up to lasting self-liberation.

This is a book for the discriminating, intelligent, and sensitive reader who is looking for *real* answers.

0-87542-223-3, 240 pgs., 5-¼ x 8, softcover $9.95

A RICH MAN'S SECRET
A Novel by Ken Roberts

Victor Truman is a modern-day guy who spends his days scanning the want ads, hoping somehow to find his "right place." He has spent years reading self-help books, sitting through "get rich quick" seminars, living on unemployment checks, practicing meditation regimens, swallowing megavitamins, listening to talk radio psychologists ... each new attempt at self-fulfillment leaving him more impoverished in spirit and wallet than he was before.

But one day, while he's retrieving an errant golf ball, Victor stumbles upon a forgotten woodland cemetery and a gravestone with the cryptic message, "Take the first step—no more, no less—and the next will be revealed." When Victor turns sleuth and discovers that this stone marks the grave of wealthy industrialist Clement Watt, whose aim was to help spiritual "orphans" find their "right place," he is compelled to follow a trail of clues that Mr. Watt seems to have left for him.

This saga crackles with the excitement of a detective story, inspires with its down-home wisdom and challenges the status quo through a penetrating look at the human comedy that Victor Truman—like all of us—is trying to understand.

1-56718-580-0, 5-¼ x 8, 208 pp., softbound **$9.95**